WRECKAGE BEGINS WITH "W"

WRECKAGE BEGINS WITH "W"

Cartoons of the Bush Administration

Drawn with all due respect by

Jeff Danziger

Foreword by

Frank Miller

Steerforth Press · Hanover, New Hampshire

For Kim

For information about permission to reproduce
selections from this book, write to:
Steerforth Press L.C., 25 Lebanon Street
Hanover, New Hampshire 03755

Danziger cartoons are syndicated by
Cartoonist and Writers Syndicate
and distributed by the

The New York Times SYNDICATE

www.nytimages.com

Library of Congress Cataloging-in-Publication Data

Danziger, Jeff.
Wreckage begins with W : cartoons of the Bush administration / drawn with
all due respect by Jeff Danziger ; foreword by Frank Miller.– 1st ed.
p. cm.
ISBN 1-58642-078-X (alk. paper)
1. Bush, George W. (George Walker), 1946–Caricatures and cartoons.
2. United States–Politics and government–2001–Caricatures and cartoons.
3. American wit and humor, Pictorial. I. Title.
E903.3.D36 2004
741.5'973–dc22
2004006626

FIRST EDITION

Book design by Peter Holm, Sterling Hill Productions

Foreword

Let us now praise angry men.

A whole lot of people are trying to give anger a bad name. In these therapeutic times, we're all supposed to think that whenever any of us are just plain pissed off about something that we're out of line. That we're being rude. That we're "experiencing negative emotions."

Give me a break. What the hell is a "negative emotion" if not a reaction to something that demands remedy? Anger can make good things happen. Anger can work wonders.

I'm not talking brainless anger here, not fits of temper, nothing hysterical. Not whiny victimhood. I'm talking focused, smart, informed anger, purposeful, guided by intelligence, prosecuted with talent. That kind of anger can work wonders — and it can make for some mighty fine cartoons.

More on the cartoons in a minute. Back to anger.

Imagine, for instance, if the Atrocity of 9/11 were called by its proper name, rather than drowned in value-neutral syrup and called "the tragic events of September 11th."

"Tragic events"? Hell, that makes it sound like it was a wildfire or an earthquake. Like it was some old Shakespeare play, or something that just kind of happened, rather than what it was: A calculated, premeditated act of mass slaughter. Of civilians. On our land. On our watch.

Imagine if a memorial were erected in downtown Manhattan. To the Atrocity. One that reflected the horror, the loss, the madness, the unleashed evil, our defiance, and, yes, our anger — rather than a pair of New Age swimming pools reflecting "absence."

Jeff Danziger might well argue with me about those last few paragraphs.

Danziger and I started arguing some time back. He was my high-school English teacher. He was also my favorite teacher. He taught me a lot. By sharing his knowledge and experience, sure, and by demanding that I read some damn good books, but more than anything, by arguing.

He came across, at times, as a cranky guy, prone to argument. I figured he was cranky because he was an old guy. Simple math tells me that he was, at the time, not even thirty.

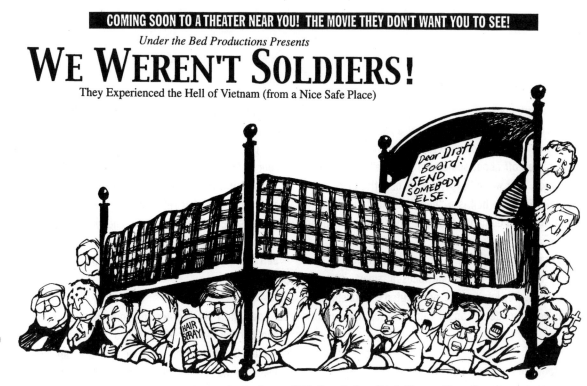

COMING SOON TO A THEATER NEAR YOU! THE MOVIE THEY DON'T WANT YOU TO SEE!

Under the Bed Productions Presents

WE WEREN'T SOLDIERS!

They Experienced the Hell of Vietnam (from a Nice Safe Place)

Starring, left to right: Danny Hastert, George Bush, George Will, Tom DeLay, Dick Cheney, Trent Lott, Dick Armey, Pat Buchanan, Newt Gingrich, Phil Gramm, William Bennett, Rush Limbaugh, Pat Robertson, Ken Starr, Dan Quayle, and Bill Clinton (as each other). Plus a cast of thousands of others!

As far as I can tell, and I hang out with the guy now and then, he hasn't calmed down much. Not much at all.

These are angry cartoons by an angry man in an angry time. You won't see any weeping Statue of Liberty in this book. This is gut-punch stuff, much needed in a time of flabby rhetoric and flabby thinking.

Sometimes they're horrifying, these cartoons are. Even humorless, when the subject demands it. Sometimes they're just plain funny. Other times the humor is exquisitely cruel. Check out how Vietnam veteran Jeff Danziger skewers nearly everybody who ever visits the White House these days with his classic, hilarious, brutal "We Weren't Soldiers."

When Danziger decides somebody's a jerk, a hypocrite, or just plain rotten, he shows little mercy. Hell, he shows no mercy whatsoever. He snaps the whip and gets the horses galloping and drags them around Troy from the back of his chariot, like he's dragging poor, bloody Hector. And he makes us laugh at the spectacle.

Danziger seems to have taken an acute dislike to the current president. To say the least. His intensity reminds me of Herblock's and Paul Conrad's historic campaign of wit against President Nixon.

Current events are bringing very good things out of Jeff Danziger. Very good, angry things.

Frank Miller
New York City
2004

NOTICE!
PLEASE WAIT HERE.
ONE OF US WILL
CONTRIBUTE SOMETHING
STUPID, REPETITIOUS
AND UNHELPFUL
ON THIS SPOT
SOON.
MR. HASTERT, MR. DeLAY
MR. DASCHLE OR
MR. FRIST
ETC.
DANZIGER

At the Ohio Clock. If you don't have much to say, say it in front of impressive architecture.

February 8, 1999

Introduction

Drawing as an expressive pastime seems to be something boys do more than girls. It is often regarded as a naughty thing, coinciding with the rigors of male puberty, as any junior-high boys' room will attest. But drawing is also a healthy outlet for boys' normally violent tendencies, available long before they learn enough vocabulary to express them in prose. Thus the same desire that urges boys to step on bugs and smash sand castles prompts them to draw wild scenes of wanton destruction, car wrecks, and airplanes aflame.

Some years ago my son's second-grade teacher, a woman with pretentions to corrective psychology, complained that he was scribbling mad scenes of war, bombing, and strafing runs that could only be the result of a troubled mind or too much violent television. Some of the drawings were accomplished to sound tracks he provided, juicy explosions and machine-gun fire, possibly even the screams of the wounded. The teacher said this was very troubling. I replied that I, myself, had drawn such pictures, and all my brothers had drawn such pictures, and we had matured as mild as milk. In fact my son is now a fairly sedate banker who rescues stranded ladybugs. Thus the healthy outlet theory is somewhat proved. None of us has done anything actually violent, although, God knows, there have been ample provocations.

Cartooning is based on drawing, even if most practitioners work hard to make it look otherwise. Cartoonists today try to produce what they think the public imagines a cartoon should be. For most this means cartoons should be badly drawn, with awkward line work and hands that look like feet. A big nose means the character is stupid, in case you couldn't figure that out yourself. With this anti-realism shorthand the field has developed some bad habits, not the least of which is the idea that if anything takes very long to draw it is suspect. There remain some towering talents, but they are few and not getting any younger. When I do see really good political artwork, I know that beyond everything else the cartoonist is enjoying himself.

The ability, in simple black and white, to make someone think they see glistening water, or the gloom of a cathedral interior, is what I value. In some cases, these effects are both contrived and derivative, a collection of tricks and techniques, but then so is most art. Some years ago I stumbled on a method of drawing a pavement surface in the rain (largely stolen from the great British cartoonist Carl

In New York City aircraft, trains, and buses are all slowed by heavy snow,
but fortunately the really critical supplies are still getting through.

February 8, 2003

Giles). I made frequent use of it, until a few months ago, when an observer, looking over my shoulder, said, "Oh, the rainy pavement again, eh?" I have been careful ever since, and you find very little rainy pavement herein. There is, however, quite a bit of my patented snow effect, and numerous, rather realistic, explosion effects. The trick, of course, is not to draw what actually happens in an explosion but to make the readers think they see an explosion.

In the past three years, my most frequently used effect has been that of generalized wreckage. By this I mean masonry strewn about, fields of rubble and twisted steel, trucks turned upside down, bullet holes stitching stucco, puddles of stagnant water in the low points. As a background this is supposed to be admonitory, telling the reader that the message is delivered ironically against obvious and profound difficulty. Wreckage, as a motif, was introduced by such magnificent talents as Honoré Daumier, Francisco José de Goya, and R. Crumb. But there has been a definite trend of late, at least at my house. We now live in a country where the visual metaphor of wreckage can be drawn as a background for all sorts of things — the economy, the political scene, the culture wars, and, of course, the real wars. It is probably unfair to place all the blame for this trend on the current administration, but they do seem to have taken the old saw about making omelettes a bit far. One could say that Mr. Bush proves the observation that for a man with a hammer everything looks like a nail.

Commenting on each successive administration means mastering the visual representations that define that presidency. In the Clinton years, one had to master backgrounds of slovenly celebration, of careless debauchery — underwear cast about and a forgotten guest passed out in the corner. Regrettably, Mr. Bush has rendered that skill all but useless. It is possible that the mood of the Bush years will prove erroneous, but I now have gotten the wreckage effect down to a science. He could claim that this is not his doing, that people are just naturally contentious and violent, and that they actually are their own worst enemies. Students of history would agree. The dispute will go on as to whether the leader incites the people or the people incite the leader. But students of political cartooning would also point out that for a man who has mastered drawing strewn masonry, twisted steel, upside-down trucks, and puddles of stagnant water, everything looks like wreckage.

An effect, if it can be called that, that I am still working on is that of soldiers, our troops, waiting and watching for the next explosion, in the blistering Iraqi heat. I have a particular feeling for these men and women, and I try to remember the poses, the worried expressions on the young troops' faces, grown rapidly older than their years, laden down by tons of crap someone sold the Pentagon. And from my time in the army in Vietnam I remember the unwarranted and unconvincing self-assurance of officers, mostly majors and above, who in truth were as confused as everyone, men trying to mimic commanders they have seen in movies.

Bill Mauldin, my hero in this effort, told me some years ago that drawing American soldiers, enlisted and officers alike, was his true love, and he couldn't get angry with them, no matter what they did. When he wanted to get mad, all he had to do was think of the politicians who had gotten the country into these wars. Well, Bill, wherever you are, not much has changed.

During the 2000 New Hampshire primary, George Bush revealed his habit of giving everyone cute nicknames. This impressed some people in the Granite State. (The bartender later married Dennis Kozlowski.)

January 20, 2000

The nature of the Taliban becomes clear, and again it is proven that men are pigs the world 'round.

January 31, 2000

The Smart Money, as usual, is way ahead of the rest of us.

Comic relief from a strange place — Burma — where twelve-year-old chain-smoking, bulletproof rebel leaders, Johnny and Luther Htoo, lead their troops to glorious defeat.

January 31, 2000

Remember him?

Putin flattens Grozny with tactics that would have made Stalin proud.

February 17, 2000

The word went out in Hanoi that former POW John McCain was going to win the New Hampshire primary.

Excuse me, uh, **OPEC**? like, these high **gasoline** prices are, like, interfering with American college students' ability to drive up and down, like, the beach? Yo, Arab dudes, we're talking **education** here, the future of, like, mankind, and whatever...

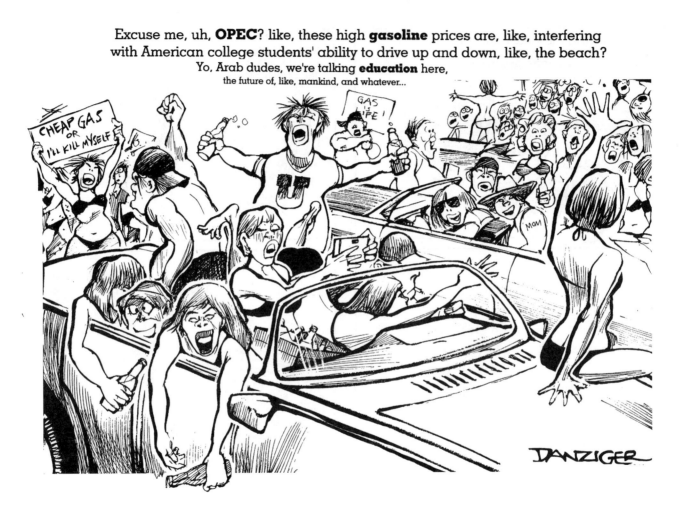

The Supreme Court steps in and strikes another blow for community standards.

March 29, 2000

Nobody promised you a rose garden.

The British Government bans the use of wafer-thin models, on the grounds that they are unhealthy.

April 18, 2000

11

Before he became a national hero, New York mayor Rudolph Giuliani was a local embarrassment.

May 10, 2000

Fires rage through Los Alamos. Later, the Park Service says that one of its people may have started it.

May 12, 2000

Bush's plan for Social Security.

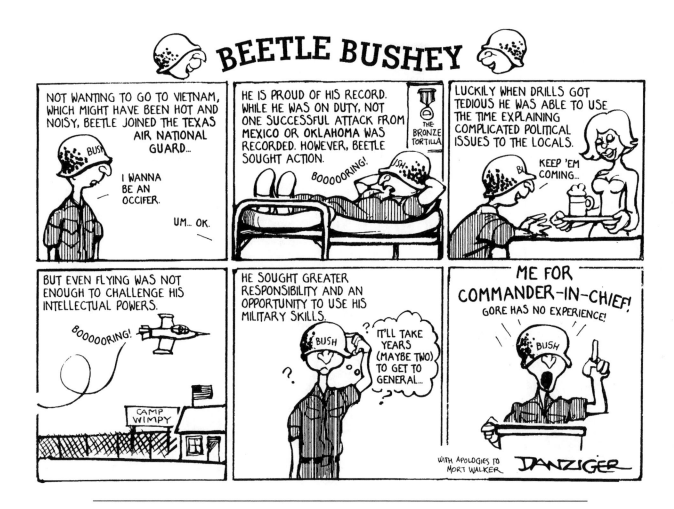

And George's murky military record becomes clearer.

Congress gives China Permanent Normal Trade status, and the Chinese celebrate their good fortune.

May 30, 2000

Toward the end of their presidential term, Bill and Hill attend the annual Gridiron festivities.

Mr. Microsoft puts on an ad blitz to convince you they just want to be your friend.

Stung by comments about his erudition, Bush decides to read some literature and stuff.

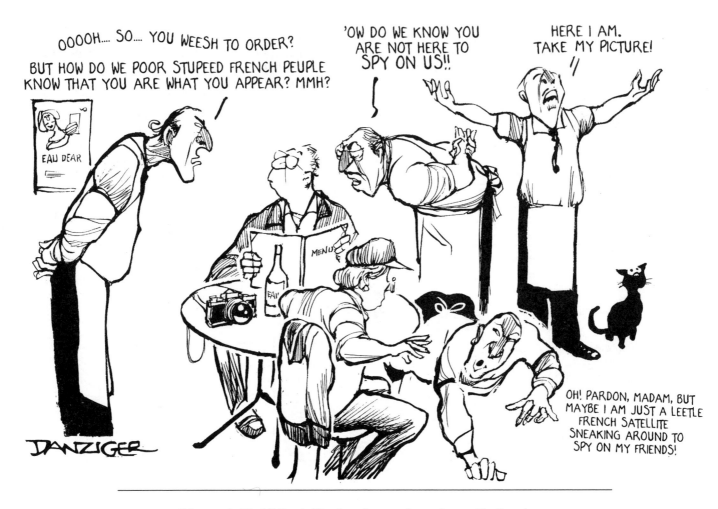

It is revealed that U.S. satellites have been spying on France. The French are understandably fromaged off and take it out on the long-suffering Paris tourist.

July 6, 2000

There's something about Texas businessmen that gives environmentalists the willies.

July 7, 2000

At the GOP convention, a whole 4 percent of the delegates are black.

Meanwhile, there's panic as Guinness sales fall among young women. The brewer tries some new tactics.

August 28, 2000

Young Republicans figure out Bush's school voucher program.

Herr Kohl's Germany celebrates ten years of reunification! But can this marriage last?

Pat Buchanan, fighting waste and government growth, accepts $12 million in federal matching funds. His lovely wife whatshername and his sister, Bob, agree.

September 18, 2000

Low point in the 2000 campaign comes when Bush calls *New York Times* reporter a body part. Good thing George is a Christian.

And finally a debate in which there is a victor.

Wall Street tripped just as Bush was suggesting people put their Social Security money there.

October 19, 2000

George and Barbara realize that W. might actually win.

Again America waded through all the negative advertising to choose Bush, Gore, Nader, or Buchanan.

The Florida recount is disorganized, idiotic, and painful.

Al ain't giving up.

The family gathers for Thanksgiving; the recount is still in progress.

Katherine Harris declares Bush the winner, or did Jim Baker?

November 27, 2000

35

The GOP recount tactics include blatant thuggery.

DANZIGER

November 28, 2000

2001: A Space Odyssey turns out to be one of the more prophetic films of our time.

November 29, 2000

OKAY, DAN....
WE ARE FOLLOWING THE YELLOW TRUCK FULL OF BALLOTS...IT'S A TRUCK... IT APPEARS TO BE YELLOW, FROM WHAT WE CAN SEE HERE.... SOMEONE IS DRIVING THIS TRUCK.. WE DON'T KNOW WHO... BUT THE TRUCK IS YELLOW. IT IS ON THE ROAD. IT IS MOVING ALONG. IN A FORWARD DIRECTION. WE WONDER WHAT THE PERSON OR PEOPLE DRIVING THIS TRUCK ARE THINKING... ARE THEY THINKING "WOW, I'VE NEVER BEEN TO TALLAHASSEE. I HOPE I DON'T GET LOST" OR ARE THEY THINKING ABOUT THE CARGO OR ABOUT LUNCH. .... AS I SAID, THE TRUCK IS GOING DOWN THE ROAD MUCH LIKE OJ SIMPSON IN HIS WHITE BRONCO, EXCEPT THAT THIS IS YELLOW WHEREAS THAT WAS WHITE AND THIS IS FLORIDA AND NOT CALIFORNIA AND THAT WAS A WHITE BRONCO AND THIS IS A YELLOW TRUCK..... THE TRUCK IS STILL YELLOW, STILL MOVING...

DANZIGER

The disputed Florida ballots are taken by truck to Tallahassee.

December 1, 2000

Florida calls a special legislative session to do what it's told. State Rep. Earle Smootly (R-Okefenokee) has to git to the capital for a special legislative session.

December 4, 2000

Conveniently, the Florida legislature has no use for the two-party system.

December 8, 2000

One of the things about the Bushes, they always write thank-you notes.

December 13, 2000

41

Minorities may protest loss of voting rights, but not the Supreme Court's minority.

December 13, 2000

Under the wire

WELL, WHERE SHOULD I START? AH, YES, I GUESS MY FIRST MEMORY IS WORKING ON EDUCATION POLICY WITH BILL IN ARKANSAS...

Bill stepped out of the shower, the beads of water glistening on his smooth white skin. He patted on some creamy sun lotion against the hot, hot Arkansas sun.
"It's hot, ain't it, darlin'?" he said, his eyes twinkling. "Yes," I said, "It's hot."

Mrs. Clinton scores an $8 million book deal. Simon and Schuster wisely assigns a ghostwriter to the project.

December 20, 2000

Meanwhile, language experts say the Queen's English has gotten closer to that of the people.

Bush's first "initiative" pays off the religious right.

Trent Lott, who like Mr. Bush was a cheerleader in college, starts the new year by condemning Mrs. Clinton.

January 3, 2001

Mr. Ashcroft lauds the Confederacy. He's not a racist. He just plays one for the Justice Department.

Senator McCain, whose mood has not improved, starts the year off with a real attitude problem.

George is sworn in.

The Clintons drop by the White House for a few things they forgot to steal
. . . eh . . . borrow . . . whatever.

Priorities

The administration slaps a ban on overseas abortion aid.

January 23, 2001

Do all faith-based groups qualify for government handouts? Hare Krishnas
would not be afraid to ask.

Finally, James Carville criticizes the Clintons.

On duty in the Balkans the U.S. Third Infantry is declared unready for combat because they have missed training because they were in a . . . er . . . war zone.

If you want some really underhanded political tricks done, call Tom "The Exterminator" DeLay.

Strom Thurmond is revived for the tax cut vote in a narrowly divided Senate.

March 12, 2001

Meanwhile, lonely in Harlem, Bill Clinton relies on his old friend Charlie Rangel to scout him up some company.

March 1, 2001

The tax cut goes through, and billions are delivered to the deserving wealthy.

A theology lesson

As Wall Street billions disappear, a certain bipartisanship emerges.

And there's strong bipartisanship on campaign finance reform!

DANZIGER

March 20, 2001

Cutbacks to IRS staff means millions go uncollected. But remaining workers
are still dedicated, vigilant, and, in the case of George Fribble, desperately
creative.

April 13, 2001

Bush administration education policy: Testing and more testing. Enough testing and they'll be begging for vouchers.

The not-yet-heroic Rudolf Giuliani has to be instructed by a judge not to bring his girlfriend over to the mayoral mansion while his wife and children are there.

May 16, 2001

A scant four months before the World Trade Towers attack, the administration announced a major antimissile defense system to protect us from the Koreans, or somebody.

May 2, 2001

Meanwhile in England, Blair wins re-election by speaking pretty much common sense. Which shocks everyone.

June 5, 2001

Tory leader William Hague resigns his post as party leader. Mrs. Thatcher
was said to help him with the wording of his announcement.

June 8, 2001

Majority Leader Trent Lott declarers war on the Democrats, but not all are ready to follow. Luckily he still has his pom-poms from back in the sixties.

June 6, 2001

Mr. Putin's patience with a free press in Russia is running out. He reverts to his early training as a Marxist-Leninist thug.

The Chinese close down Internet cafés.

July 23, 2001

But they are accused of fostering an organ-harvesting industry in livers, kidneys, and whatever else can be excised.

July 2, 2001

The U.S. Army gives all troops cool black berets to wear as a morale builder. The morale of Charlie Company's KP squad goes way up! Later, it is revealed that the berets are made in China.

June 15, 2001

Gone

July 6, 2001

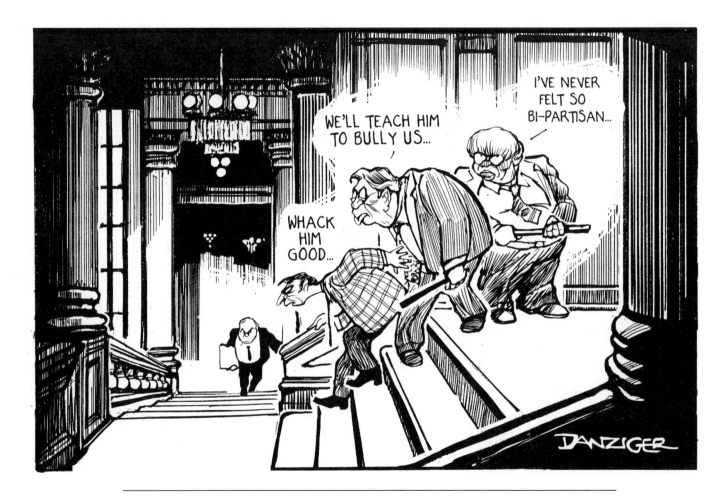

Congressmen DeLay, Armey, and Hastert attack the McCain-Feingold bill,
especially that unpatriotic McCain.

July 9, 2001

Chandra Levy goes missing and Congressman Condit is the suspect. The nation is riveted to the story, or else.

July 9, 2001

The White House announces that its main contact man to the Mideast oil states will be the president's father.

Religious fundamentalists force the administration to stop stem-cell research
on the grounds that cells have souls.

July 18, 2001

Rupert Murdoch takes his new wife, young enough to be his daugh — er, granddaughter — out to dinner.

Bush spends more time away from the White House than any recent president.

A certain pattern is detected in Bush's speeches.

Jesse Helms and Strom Thurmond are living proof that only the good die young.

And then, all hell broke loose.

September 11, 2001

The New York spirit

September 12, 2001

The undoubted low point of Bush leadership. Bush lets himself be flown to Nebraska for his own security. Giuliani leads the nation.

September 13, 2001

How to get even with Afghanistan?

Problems emerge in the Alliance.

September 18, 2001

Our Saudi allies dig in for the long fight ahead.

October 3, 2001

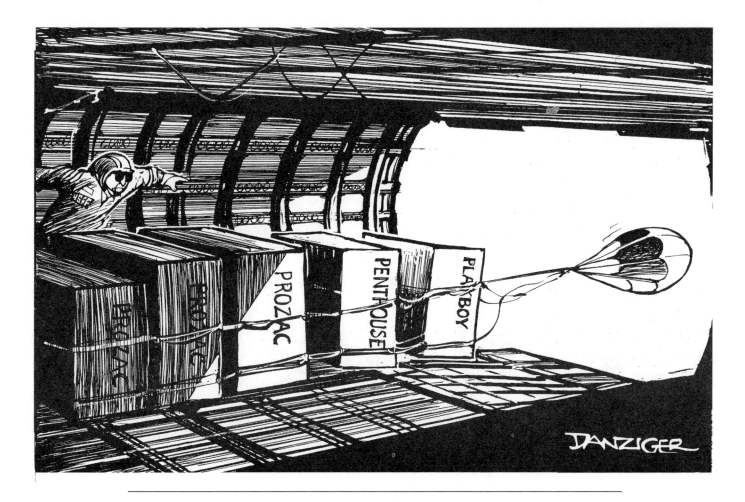

Psychological operations over Taliban territory

October 16, 2001

News for Osama

Miranda Rights for Osama

October 10, 2001

And in the middle of everything, the great old man leaves us.

Television news marches on. And yes, sadly, they did find Chandra.

October 17, 2001

95

U.S. military advisers, all starched and shaved, show up to get the anti-Taliban forces organized.

Ann Coulter is fired from the *National Review On-Line* and decides to take matters into her own hands. Somewhere over Afghanistan she bails out in search of the evildoers!

October 4, 2001

The Pentagon hires Hollywood scriptwriters to imagine terror scenarios to prepare for. This actually did happen, at great cost to the taxpayer; it is not some cartoonist's concoction.

October 19, 2001

Interrogation

October 24, 2001

Two, or was it three, letters containing possible anthrax are received by senators. Capitol closes down. Panic ensues. Staff sent home.

October 23, 2001

While everyone is distracted, Messers. Armey, Hastert, and DeLay risk life
and limb to rob the place blind.

October 25, 2001

The administration admits that the War on Terror may take longer than previously thought.

October 29, 2001

The country's shoddy treatment of its veterans is covered up.

October 31, 2001

Meanwhile, the Clintons are making so much money that it's worth it for them to stay married. If you can imagine that large a sum . . .

The administration offers a $25 million reward for bin Laden, which poses a dilemma for the faithful.

Monty Python alive and well in Afghanistan

Our motto

Ashcroft refuses to let the FBI use gun registration data. The NRA wins again.

Bush pulls out of the ABM treaty unilaterally. Who needs it?

Mr. Putin is smelling sweeter than ever.

Airline security should be fun!

There's millions in savings for the British if they join the Euro, but . . .

The Best Little Piano Player in Texas

January 14, 2002

Dick Cheney is keeping the truth in an undisclosed location.

A Texas businessman prays.

February 1, 2002

America is on guard!

IF YOUR RETIREMENT PLANS CHANGE...

Listen, if your stocks are wiped out by crooked executives, accountants and politicians, don't worry. You can spend your remaining years meeting people and performing a useful service at minimum wage. You may even get robbed again.

Mr. Bush explains to the Chinese why certain nations are on the Axis of Evil list.

Mr. Bush kicks off a campaign fund-raising tour by signing the McCain-Feingold legislation.

March 29, 2002

Mr. Sharon and Mr. Arafat are just never going to work together.

The American Catholic hierarchy is left to develop its own methods for dealing with abusive priests.

Slowly, slowly, the mills of theology catch up with the times.

Mr. Bush meets with new Chinese leader Hu Jiniao and demonstrates his grasp of international trade.

May 2, 2002

123

Ozzy Osbourne's odd popularity means he is now seen at Republican socials.

Once a Democrat program, farm subsidies prove very resistant to GOP budget-cutters.

Martha Stewart runs afoul of the SEC. Great decorating minds jump forward in fantasy.

June 13, 2002

The government calls on citizens everywhere to be on the lookout. Even in Los Angeles.

Safeguarding our freedoms

June 24, 2002

The FBI starts raiding U.S. libraries. Many librarians don't cooperate.

The Supreme Court approves vouchers for religious schools, forgetting that
Islam is also a religion.

July 2, 2002

Victory at sea

Young Republicans have to start somewhere.

Congress plays with rules to limit profiteering on the War on Terror.

July 23, 2002

Things go from bad to worse in the airline business.

In all the confusion Jean Chretien, prime minister of the country north of here, announces he'll resign.

As the war talk heats up, Colin Powell, an actual war veteran, waits to play the Powell card.

Condoleezza Rice, a gifted pianist, plays a little seasonal ditty she composed herself.

Later on we find out that the decision had been made months ago.

Americans have other worries, like, why are our kids so fat?

America's youth shows its patriotism.

September 4, 2002

DANZIGER

September 17, 2002

142

The deal

The vacuum left by Martha Stewart is filled by another determined woman.

September 26, 2002

The U.S. economy dives, support of the war follows.

September 26, 2002

Mr. Rumsfeld gases his own people.

Captain AWOL

Closing hours are extended in British pubs to prevent violence in the street.
And it works!

Colin Powell talks the Chicken Hawks into giving the inspection team one more chance.

November 18, 2002

Bush asks Henry Kissinger to head a panel looking into the causes of terrorism.

Henry Kissinger agrees to lead the September 11 investigation no matter where it leads. On second thought, he drops quietly out.

December 2, 2002

Senator Lott first says retiring Senator Strom Thurmond should have been president, then apologizes, then apologizes to his constituents for apologizing. Nothing works.

December 12, 2002

Mutually assured madness

December 13, 2002

Yale's Skull & Bone men hear that Bush now authorizes the CIA to kill people.

The new Homeland Security Department soaks up billions that would have been otherwise wasted.

December 30, 2002

The U.S. Air Force admits that it has been distributing amphetamines to fighter pilots.

January 5, 2003

The Republican base weighs in on overpopulation and reproductive health.

And a fine view of Central Park

Venus and Serena Williams are making billions with a "b" hitting a ball around.

Tony Blair samples public opinion before visiting Mr. Bush. You have to know what public opinion is before you can ignore it.

January 31, 2003

Back at the Pentagon, some doubt Mr. Rumsfeld's leadership.

Mr. Rumsfeld, expanding his field of insult, says Germany and France are "Old Europe," unlike our ally, England. Here, Londoners bask in newfound modernity.

The one man who should remember that the reasons for going to war are always suspect seems to have political amnesia.

February 6, 2003

Meanwhile, the Democrats gather to regroup, and . . . eh . . . gather . . .

It's sweeps week! Did we mention it's sweeps week?

February 23, 2003

And Dan Rather gets to interview Saddam Hussein.

Nevertheless, Mr. Bush will have his war.

February 17, 2003

Mr. Rumsfeld visits the Phillipines to try to get their help in the war on terror.

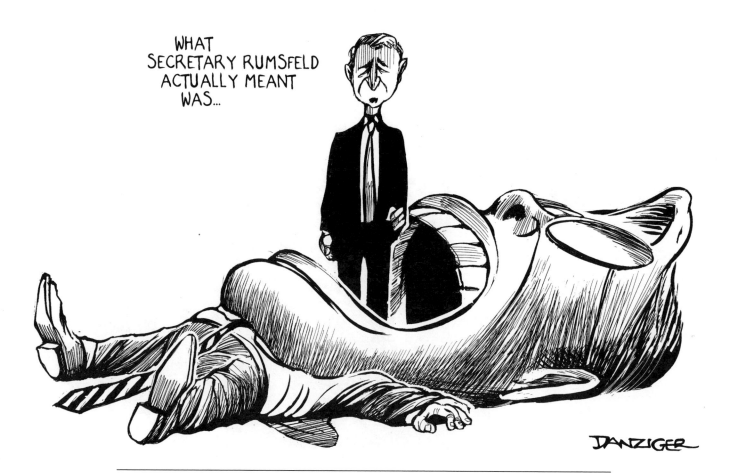

Mr. Bush has to clarify statements from Mr. Rumsfeld, giving the impression that he is in charge. Or that someone is.

March 12, 2003

Our strongest ally. Maybe our only ally.

March 21, 2003

On the road to Baghdad

March 24, 2003

The White House admits that the war may take longer than originally predicted.

Richard Perle is forced to resign a Pentagon post because it is noticed that
a number of his extracurricular activities do indeed make his ass look fat.

March 28, 2003

In early horror, U.S. bombs kill a boy's mother, and he loses the arms with which he was holding her.

April 16, 2003

One Dixie Chick criticizes Bush, and right-wing radio punishes everyone.

With apologies to Margaret Bourk-White

May 13, 2003

Another Karl Rove production

DANZIGER

Prop gun

May 5, 2003

Mr. Rumsfeld explains.

May 6, 2003

Teaching democracy to Iraqis

Guiding principles of the Cheney administration

Did we mention that Tom Delay was an exterminator by trade?

Former diplomat Paul Bremer senses that diplomacy isn't working in Baghdad.

May 21, 2003

New Treasury Captain John Snow can't wait to demonstrate our new "strong dollar" policy.

May 20, 2003

Warren Buffett says tax cuts are not a good idea. But what does he know?

May 29, 2003

Bush wants to give Murdoch permission to own more of the U.S. media. Evidently Jesus would want to see more of the Murdoch formula in American journalism.

June 3, 2003

Mr. Bush's Israel policy has everyone confused except him.

The problem

June 13, 2003

The Clintons explained

Hollywood wants Jessica Lynch's story, which, as it turned out, was . . . a story.

June 17, 2003

191

Only people with long memories (three months at least) will remember that the timing of the war was to avoid the Iraq summer heat. One hundred and fifteen in the shade.

June 17, 2003

Same-sex marriages, or something, are legalized for everyone in Canada.

June 20, 2003

A month later: Canada leads, Texas follows. A local court says the state must allow marriage between everybody.

Strom Thurmond and Lester Maddox both leave the building within weeks of each other.

July 1, 2003

The Bush administration pushes abstinence as a way to counter AIDS, while cutting money for family planning. The message is carried to Brazil, which faces an HIV pandemic, and goes over well.

July 15, 2003

As the killing goes on, the guy who pressured the CIA into providing false intelligence makes himself scarce.

July 17, 2003

Mr. Bush and Mr. Cheney talk it over.

From out of nowhere (Vermont, actually) comes someone named Howard Dean, who, it is later revealed, actually grew up in the rural reaches of New York's Park Avenue.

July 10, 2003

PUSH ON!

DANZIGER

During Vietnam, a Pete Seeger song, "Knee Deep in the Big Muddy," answered Johnson's claim that all we had to do was stay the course and the war would be won. Mark Twain said, "History doesn't repeat itself, but it rhymes."

July 2, 2003

Another month in Iraq

July 9, 2003

Meanwhile, in California, everyone is running for governor.

U.S. military death toll continues to mount.

Road map for peace talks break down almost immediately.

On the beach

Harley-Davidson celebrates 100 years of making the country's best-loved
motorcycles. Some would say too well loved.

August 28, 2003

Where will the tax cuts be spent? On things made here in the United States, so that U.S. jobs are created? Or in some electronics factory in far-off China?

September 2, 2003

Bush raised record amounts of campaign funds over the summer but couldn't attend GI funerals.

California courts threaten to stop the recall election. Republicans, with absolutely no sense of irony, object.

"Survivor"

If we can shuck this nation-building stuff off on the UN, how much control do we give them?

Secretary Powell visits Baghdad for a report from Paul Bremer.

September 16, 2003

Messers. Blair, Chirac, and Schroeder discuss life in general. The quote is from Monty Python.

While the economy burns

September 19, 2003

George Bush's America

October 7, 2003

A new celebrity political party! Parties should be fun!

Mr. Rush Limbaugh, a victim, is interrupted on his way to a Druggies Anonymous meeting.

October 15, 2003

Mr. Putin picks Mr. Kadyrov to win in Chechnya's Russian-approved election.
And we are back in the USSR!

October 6, 2003

Remember, you've hated the Turks for centuries. You've only hated us for a few lousy years.

The White House reacts to criticism that Bush never attends GI funerals.

Millions of jobs disappear while the White House concentrates on wars.

Prince Charles fights rumors that he has a boyfriend.

November 10, 2003

In a political departure from accepted philosophy, the White House agrees
to protect the steel industry, which just happens to be located in states
they need to win in November.

November 11, 2003

No one wants credit for claiming victory.

With all due respect to Milton Caniff

November 12, 2003

227

Labor Secretary Chao said that the stock market was the "final arbiter" in the recovery.

November 14, 20035

Meanwhile, the press is diverted from the war by Michael Jackson's sexual proclivities.

November 20, 2003

The Massachusetts Supreme Court says gays have the right to marry, something Rockwell never foresaw.

November 20, 2003

Mr. Kerry gets lots of advice in New Hampshire. Lots. Tons.

November 24, 2003

If you want decent health care, get elected.

Mr. Bush wows the troops by showing up in Baghdad for Thanksgiving. With a fake turkey. With the press. For two hours.

November 28, 2003

High jinks at the Boeing Company include sweet deals for all sorts of administration biggies, including the king of the neoconmen, Richard Perle.

Our ally Mr. Putin, emerging democrat, completes his grip on the Russian press in the best Stalinist tradition.

Karl Rove plans to McGovernize Howard Dean. Later, Howard beat him to it.

December 11, 2003

We got him! Now what the hell do we do with him?

Checkmate. But the game goes on and on . . .

Lesser Known Firsts of the Wright Brothers

Several days after their historic first flight
the Wright brothers take another flight
during which Orville discovers a
couple of sandwiches in his pocket.

America celebrates the centenary of the Wright Brothers' flight.

December 17, 2003

If **Strom Thurmond** had been black and had crossed the color line. . .

We find that Strom Thurmond, now safely dead, had a black mistress with whom he had a child.

December 18, 2003

Drug Industry Secretary Tommy Thompson moves to make Canadian drugs harder for Americans to get.

December 22, 2003

Our old friend Slobo, on trial for war crimes, is re-elected by Serbs.

December 30, 2003

Kerry and Lieberman over a cup. For a time, Dean appears to be unstoppable.

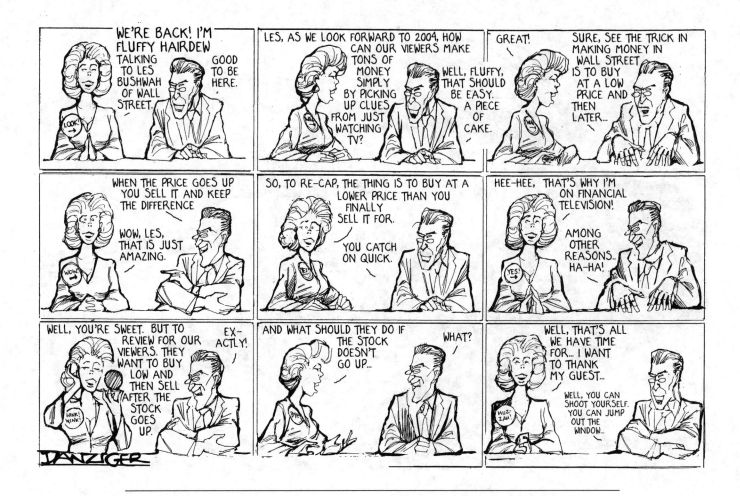

Television puts its mind on hold for the New Year.

"No Child Left Whatever" is the administration's policy, and even that is underfunded.

January 7, 2004

Things get crazier. Bush proposes illegal alien workers get to stay while new regulations are strengthened for those attempting legal entry.

President Bush attended fund-raising dinners in his quest
for a record $200,000,000.00 in election contributions.

Meanwhile...

The Islamic supremos in Iran kick a bunch of candidates out of the elections. What is this, Florida?

More policy from outer space. Mr. Bush announces that we're going to the moon, Mars, another galaxy far, far away!

January 19, 2004

Corporate farms feed guts and brains back to otherwise vegetarian cattle, allowing mad cow disease to spread.

On the campaign trail, Al Sharpton spends lavishly — up to $2,000 per night
for the best room in the house.

January 15, 2004

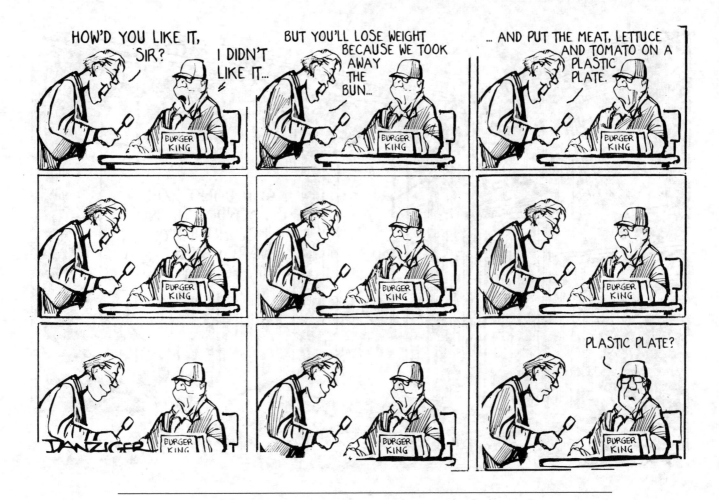

Burger King fights the war on fat. Hey, who's looking out for you?

Right after the proper sorrow on MLK Day, Mr. Bush slides another right-wing judge onto the bench.

The totally inexplicable Iowa caucuses depend on weather, cookies, and, oh, yes, politics.

January 18, 2004

The Iraq situation worsens, so bad in fact that the White House tries to suck in the UN.

Airborne!

If not the worst State of the Union speech, it was one of them. And what
was that blather about steroids?

January 19, 2004

YOU'RE THE FRONT RUNNER...

LOSE THE BIKE.

DANZIGER

Mrs. Kerry never did like that damn Harley.

January 21, 2004

Dean commits whacki-whacki, sort of like hiri-kiri.

We begin to suspect that Senator Edwards just doesn't understand the situation.

Justice Antonin Scalia goes duck hunting with Uncle Dick, who is in a case before the Supreme Court. Conflict, schmonflict.

U.S. deaths in Iraq exceed 500, occurring at a higher rate than in the early days of Vietnam.

Germans and French ignore their own debt limit rules on the euro.

Bienvenidos to unemployment!

New Hampshire totals up a small fortune off their primary.

January 26, 2004

Mr. Powell expresses concern about an authoritarian Pootey-poot.

January 27, 2004

Elaine Chao's Labor Department counsels employers on how to get out of paying overtime.

January 28, 2004

Before We Have Democracy in Iraq We Gotta Talk to These Guys!

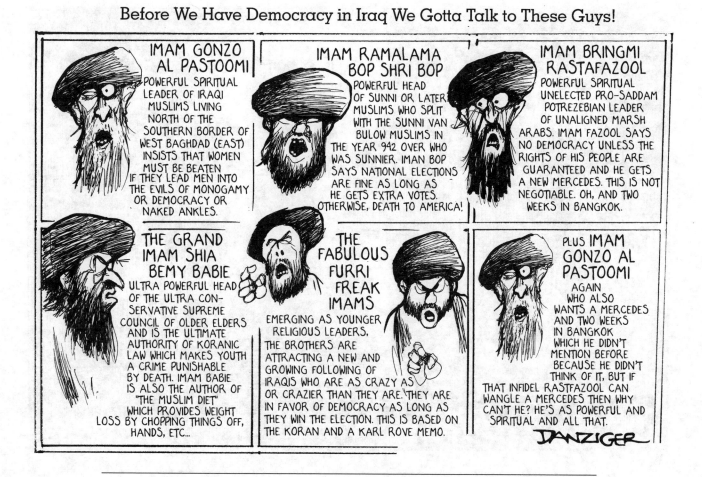

IMAM GONZO AL PASTOOMI POWERFUL SPIRITUAL LEADER OF IRAQI MUSLIMS LIVING NORTH OF THE SOUTHERN BORDER OF WEST BAGHDAD (EAST) INSISTS THAT WOMEN MUST BE BEATEN IF THEY LEAD MEN INTO THE EVILS OF MONOGAMY OR DEMOCRACY OR NAKED ANKLES.

IMAM RAMALAMA BOP SHRI BOP POWERFUL HEAD OF SUNNI OR LATER MUSLIMS WHO SPLIT WITH THE SUNNI VAN BULOW MUSLIMS IN THE YEAR 942 OVER WHO WAS SUNNIER. IMAN BOP SAYS NATIONAL ELECTIONS ARE FINE AS LONG AS HE GETS EXTRA VOTES. OTHERWISE, DEATH TO AMERICA!

IMAM BRINGMI RASTAFAZOOL POWERFUL SPIRITUAL UNELECTED PRO-SADDAM POTREZEBIAN LEADER OF UNALIGNED MARSH ARABS. IMAM FAZOOL SAYS NO DEMOCRACY UNLESS THE RIGHTS OF HIS PEOPLE ARE GUARANTEED AND HE GETS A NEW MERCEDES. THIS IS NOT NEGOTIABLE. OH, AND TWO WEEKS IN BANGKOK.

THE GRAND IMAM SHIA BEMY BABIE ULTRA POWERFUL HEAD OF THE ULTRA CON-SERVATIVE SUPREME COUNCIL OF OLDER ELDERS AND IS THE ULTIMATE AUTHORITY OF KORANIC LAW WHICH MAKES YOUTH A CRIME PUNISHABLE BY DEATH. IMAM BABIE IS ALSO THE AUTHOR OF "THE MUSLIM DIET" WHICH PROVIDES WEIGHT LOSS BY CHOPPING THINGS OFF, HANDS, ETC...

THE FABULOUS FURRI FREAK IMAMS EMERGING AS YOUNGER RELIGIOUS LEADERS, THE BROTHERS ARE ATTRACTING A NEW AND GROWING FOLLOWING OF IRAQIS WHO ARE AS CRAZY AS OR CRAZIER THAN THEY ARE. THEY ARE IN FAVOR OF DEMOCRACY AS LONG AS THEY WIN THE ELECTION. THIS IS BASED ON THE KORAN AND A KARL ROVE MEMO.

PLUS IMAM GONZO AL PASTOOMI AGAIN WHO ALSO WANTS A MERCEDES AND TWO WEEKS IN BANGKOK WHICH HE DIDN'T MENTION BEFORE BECAUSE HE DIDN'T THINK OF IT, BUT IF THAT INFIDEL RASTFAZOOL CAN WANGLE A MERCEDES THEN WHY CAN'T HE? HE'S AS POWERFUL AND SPIRITUAL AND ALL THAT.

DANZIGER

The United States tries to rush sovereignity in Iraq but runs into objections from religious self-dealers. Who ARE these guys?

January 28, 2004

267

The Hutton Report says Blair is not at fault in the Kelly suicide, prompting the undecided to decide that, of course, he absolutely is.

Brazilian Border Police start fingerprinting Americans. Meanwhile the White House goes off on a marriage tangent.

How poor was **John Edwards** when he was growing up?

Well, pictures ain't gonna tell you no lie...

with apologies to Dorothea Lange

Senator Edwards repeats that he was born poor, and repeats, and repeats. And here's proof!

February 2, 2004

Whose fault is it that there are no weapons of mass you-know-what?

February 3, 2004

The other day,
upon the stair,
I met a man
who wasn't there.

He wasn't there
again today.
I wish, I wish
he'd go away.

Ah, Vietnam — the gift that keeps on giving. (With thanks to Hughes Mearns.)

The forge

February 4, 2004

Senator Edwards' bus cruises through a southern town.

The Really Big Dig. Republicans start their opposition research right in Kerry's backyard.

February 10, 2004

North Korea's Dear Whatsis begins to worry about his own WMD.

Muhamar Khadaffy, Moo to his friends, gives up weapons of mass destruction to rejoin the civilized. Oddly, he actually did have some.

February 10, 2004

The Snow effect

February 11, 2004

Mr. Bush's dental records are dragged out to prove he actually did show up for the Alabama National Guard. Isn't that the same guy who examined Saddam?

February 12, 2004

Paris erupts in religious conflict over headscarves. French students take to the barricades.

February 13, 2004

Matt Drudge breaks the story of the century, that Kerry had an affair. The girl
in questions says . . . ah . . . didn't happen. Never mind. Developing . . .

February 13, 2004

Pentagon stops paying Halliburton because of overcharges for food and gasoline.

The Outsourcerer's Apprenctice

The administration floats the Mickey Mouse idea that shipping jobs overseas is actually good.

February 17, 2004

Some Republicans say dump Cheney, but Mr. Bush is loyal.

Nobody asked the horse.

The mayor of San Francisco starts issuing marriage licenses to same-sex couples. Well, it takes your mind off the war.

Kerry's famous question comes back.

Desperate for spiritual guidance and popcorn, Americans flood to see Mel Gibson's Christ.

February 23, 2004

Nader announces that he is in the running. Democrats bring out their secret weapon.

February 23, 2004

We're all getting married now! Two Vermont ladies celebrate their love by getting united, not only with each other, but with their two dogs, three cats, a parrot, several kittens, an ewe, a lamb, an incredibly ugly table lamp, and a six-pack of Molson Export

March 21, 2003

Some suggest that the cure for gay marriage is . . . gay marriage.

Alan Greenspan trifles with Social Security, the so-called third rail of American politics.

March 1, 2004

Russian politics starts to look awfully familiar.

March 1, 2004

293

Afloat in the political Mekong Delta, John Edwards gives up his quest.

March 2, 2004

The price of gasoline touches two dollars a gallon, which is mighty tough on the Nascar dads.

March 8, 2004

And what's a world at war if Haiti isn't going crazy?

Federal law says all weapons must be shipped in checked baggage. Karen Hughes arrives in Washington.

March 9, 2004

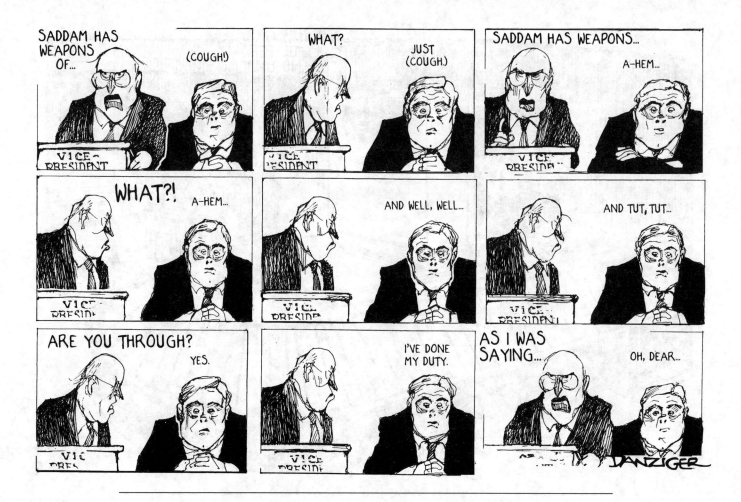

FBI director George Tenet says that, yes, he did caution Mr. Cheney that there was no proof of WMD. Ahem . . .

March 10, 2004

The FCC threatens massive fines if the radio stations don't clean up their acts.

March 14, 2004

Programming jobs shipped wholesale to India and China. Martin Niemoller's classic quotation resonates.

March 14, 2004

The administration gets caught sending out ads for their new health insurance scheme that are designed to look and sound like real news reports.

Terrorists attack Madrid, and Spain says it will pull out of Iraq. Will Mr. Bush speak to these summer soldiers in their native tongue?

And what's a world at war if the Serbs and Albanians can't start killing each other?

Karl Rove plans to make this campaign all about Bush's strong leadership in time of war.

Flak vests are in short supply in Iraq. Some parents actually send vests to their sons and daughters.

March 24, 2004

Give a judge enough rope and he'll hang himself.

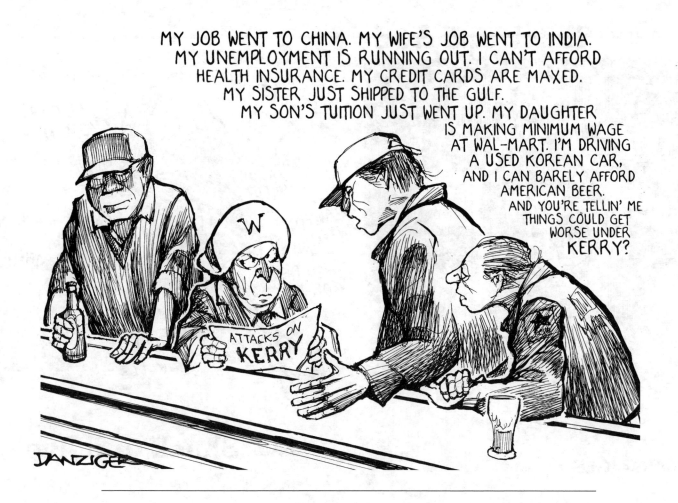

Remember, things can *always* get worse.

March 24, 2004

307

THEN: **Shock and Awe**

NOW: **Shuck and Jive**

DANZIGER

February 9, 2004

308